1 MONTH OF
FREE
READING

at

www.ForgottenBooks.com

By purchasing this book you are eligible for one month membership to ForgottenBooks.com, giving you unlimited access to our entire collection of over 1,000,000 titles via our web site and mobile apps.

To claim your free month visit:
www.forgottenbooks.com/free745776

ISBN 978-0-484-43295-5
PIBN 10745776

and 155 "no." That this negative vote was complicated with other questions, and did not indicate opposition to extending a call to Dr. Barbour, was pleasantly shown when the vote was taken to make the call unanimous. Then there were only fifteen dissentients, and it is likely that these were not opposed to Dr. Barbour. The call therefore may properly be considered as practically unanimous. Dr. Barbour's attitude with reference to this whole matter strikes us as admirable. He has not given the slightest indication of a desire to become the pastor of Tremont Temple. On the contrary, it has been evident to him from the first that this is a work only to be undertaken under the gravest

REV. C. A. BARBOUR, D. D., '88

sense of duty. His position has been that he would not shrink from the fulfilment of any clear duty, but that his own preference would be to remain in the happy and successful work in which he is engaged in Rochester. We have the brightest anticipations of Dr. Barbour's success if he comes to Boston. But that will not depend wholly upon him. It will largely depend on the co-operation of the members of Tremont Temple Church with the new pastor. And we are satisfied that there is so much genuine Christian spirit in that great congregation, so much willingness to forego personal opinion, and so much earnest desire to promote the interests of the cause of Christ as represented by this church, that Dr. Barbour will find a congregation cordially united in making this church even a greater power in the community."

Announcement was made, March 29, of Dr. Barbour's declination of the call.

1891

Ernest A. Hicks writes from Tunis under date of February 24; "The BROWN ALUMNI MONTHLY has been such a treat while I have been abroad this time that I think you should know what a good work you have started. The *Brown Magazine* was a

worthy enterprise, and I for one, was very sor see it merged with the *Brunonian*, but it di have the interest for the alumni that the new azine has. Mrs. Hicks and I are having a time in northern Africa, where we are spendir winter. I am taking a six months' vacatior Mrs. Hicks is painting pictures. Tunis is a fascinating place. Perhaps you will be inter in one or two snapshots from my camera. to complete success for the ALUMNI MONTH

Mr. Hicks was editor-in-chief of the *Brown azine* in his senior year. The editor of the AL MONTHLY shares his regrets regarding it.

Two articles by Professor Edwin G. Dext the University of Illinois have recently bee printed in pamphlet form. One of them er "High-grade men in College and Out," appear the March number of *The Popular Science Mo* 1903; the other entitled "Training for the Le Professions" was contributed to *The Educa Review* for January, 1903.

Frank E. Winsor, C. E., until recently di engineer on construction of the western aqu for the Metropolitan Water Works of Bosto been appointed assistant engineer by the co son on additional water supply for New city, with offices at 2023 Park Row building.

1892

The Macmillan Company's March list o books announces a new volume in the Mac pocket classics series by Professor Marsl Brown of New York University. It is e Epoch Making Papers in American History, intended for use in the public schools.

1894

Clayton S. Cooper, Bible department retary of the student Young Men's Christian ciations of the United States and Canada, w duct Bible study institutes among the colle Massachusetts and Rhode Island under the tion of the state executive committee. H visit the Boston associations April 20 and associations in Worcester Academy and Wo Polytechnic Institute May 7, and the fol week will be at Amherst, Williams, Brov Massachusetts State College.

1897

Gregory D. Walcott has completed his w assistant pastor at the Central Congreg Church in Providence.

1899

The engagement of William E. Farnha Miss Mary F. Moore of New Bedford is annc Mr. Farnham is now an electrical enginee the American Telephone and Telegraph Boston. His home address is 477 Massac avenue.

1902

Miss Florence Brandenburg has returne abroad and is now in Boston. Her addre Whiting street, Roxbury, Mass.

1903

The engagement of Jerry Dearborne I New York, 1903, and Miss Helen Whitm Providence, 1903, has been announced. M left college in 1901 and entered business in new York.

THE
BROWN ALUMNI MONTHLY

Vol. III   Providence, R. I., May, 1903   No. 10

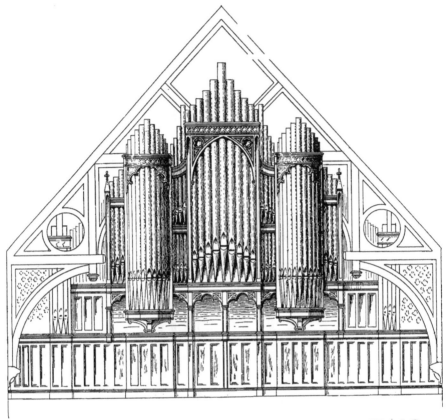

THE NEW ORGAN FOR SAYLES HALL

THE organ which Lucian Sharpe of the class of 1893 has given to the university in memory of his parents will be fully constructed and in position by commencement. The sketch above shows the case and pipes in elevation. The organ will be a magnificent instrument, the largest in the state, and will be a potent medium of culture in the university.

As was stated last month, the contract for the construction of the organ was made with the Hutchings-Votey Organ Company of Boston, builders of the new organs for Yale and Vassar and of the organ in Symphony Hall, Boston. It will be a large three-manual instrument with fifty-one speaking stops, twelve in the great organ, sixteen in the swell organ, eleven in the choir organ, and twelve in the pedal organ. The swell and choir organs will be enclosed in separate swell boxes. Besides the fifty-one speaking stops there will be forty-four mechanical accessories.

An analysis of the scheme for pitch shows

Pitch	No. of stops	No. of pipes.
32'	1	32
16'	11	497
8'	27	1,531
4'	6	337
2⅔'	1	61
2'	3	183
mixtures	2	488 (8 ranks)

Speaking stops, 51   Pipes, 3,129

A grouping of the stops according to tone families shows

Diapasons......................	17 stops
Flutes........................	15 "
Strings.......................	10 "
Reeds	9 "
Total......................	51 '

The action of the instrument is of the type known as electro-pneumatic, which not only insures an instantaneous response, but allows greater freedom in the location of the mechanical parts of the organ than any other method of construction. The current is supplied by two sets of storage batteries charged by the electric light circuit through a series of lamps and so arranged that either set may be used at will. The cells have a capacity of 10 amperes at 8 volts for 8 hours. The organ uses only about 3 or 4 amperes at about 6 volts.

The wind chests are of the individual valve type, i. e., there is a valve and complete wind supply for each pipe and so delicate is the adjustment they admit of and so prompt their action that any pipe will speak many times faster than any organist can manipulate the keys. The wind is supplied by a bellows 14 x 6'9" with three square feeders and operated by a two-horse power slow-speed motor, which is governed automatically by a large fireproof rheostat. From this bellows the wind is conducted into smaller reservoirs, one for each division of the organ, and from these small reservoirs to the chests. This arrangement makes the wind absolutely steady and permits different pressures to be used on different stops.

During the past month a new gallery has been built in Sayles Hall in order to afford adequate space and support for the new organ. These alterations have been made under the direction of Stone, Carpenter & Willson, the well-known architectural firm of Providence. The new gallery is erected

at a level of more than two feet below the former one and extends six and a half feet farther into the hall. Unlike the old gallery, the new one will have a projecting centre. This will consist of a square projection of four feet and in the centre of the front a further octagonal projection of two and a half feet. The new gallery will have in front of the organ about the same seat-

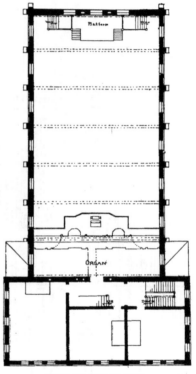

PLAN OF SAYLES HALL
Showing Balcony and Second Floor

ing room as the balcony had. There will be room for three rows of seats for the choir and space for the key desk in front of the central part of the organ.

The case of the organ is of antique oak, somewhat darker than the oak in the hall.

As the weight of the organ is to be not less than twenty-five tons, a frame work of two fifteen-inch and twelve nine-inch rolled steel beams resting upon the brick walls of hall and on two cast iron columns, was erected for the support of the gallery. In taking down the gallery-front great care was exercised not to injure it in order that it may be reset as the front of the new gallery.

The accompanying plan of the second floor of Sayles Hall shows by dotted lines the position of the trusses. It will be observed in the plan, and in the elevation, that the centre of the first outstanding truss will be included within the organ while the hammer beams on either side will be exposed to view. Access to the gallery will be had through the organ from the doorway in the second story hall and by doors in the panel work of the organ-front.

PROFESSOR FRANCIS WAYLAND, LL. D.

By Theodore Salisbury Woolsey

Professor of International Law in Yale University

THE double debt of Yale to Brown, for two Brunonians who have adorned and conspicuously served for many years the former's departments of theology and law, has been often noticed. The ready transfer of allegiance from one collegiate mother to another, so common amongst all our institutions of learning, should be a useful commentary upon much of the petty academic rivalry which is rife. We are all, in a large sense, members one of another. Phillips Brooks once said of church denominations, including his own, that each was entitled to the family name, but not to the exclusion of the others. So it is with our universities; their objects are alike noble ; their training entitles their sons all alike to the family name of alumnus; where they learn and where they teach is really only a question of how they can best serve their day and generation. And so we see the methods and ideals and traditions of one university mingled with those of another to their common benefit ; each rises up and calls the others blessed.

A year ago Dr. Walker printed in these pages a brief review of the life and services of Professor Fisher, who had but lately laid down the active duties of his office. To-day it falls to my lot to attempt the same characterization of Professor Wayland, whose resignation, after thirty years of service, is near at hand.

Francis Wayland is in a peculiar sense a son of Brown, for although born in Boston, August 23, 1826, the very next year saw him in Providence, and here he grew to youth and manhood under the double influence of Brown and of Brown's great president, graduating in 1846, when President Wayland had still nine years of office.

The son of a college president in a college community has rather a curious position. His behavior and his scholarship must both be above suspicion. In fact I think it is generally assumed that the latter is an inheritable quality. With certain unquestioned advantages from the father's walk and conversation, his friends, his table talk, his knowledge of men and things, the son has yet the sense of never meeting expectations, of hopeless inferiority from his earliest years.

That Francis Wayland, the son, should leave his father's roof, and turn his back on the academic life which surely had an opening for him, was then a not unnatural severance of the social bonds referred to, a wish to make unshadowed his own career. The profession which he chose was the law. The training for it he got, first in a Providence office, then in the Harvard Law School, where he spent a year, finally with Ashmun and Chapman in Springfield. After these four years of study he was admitted to the bar in Boston and established himself for practice in Worcester in the autumn of 1850, with a clear appreciation of Worcester's promise amongst the New England cities. There he lived and worked for nearly eight years, and built up a good practice. He did something better still, for October 6, 1857, at the age of thirty-one, he married Miss Martha Reed of New Haven. Incidentally this act was the cause of a change of residence. For Mrs. Wayland was an only child and at the instance of her parents the move to New Haven was made. Before settling down for permanent work, however, there ensued a residence of two years in Europe, beginning in 1859. Both in Worcester and in New Haven Mr. Wayland was active in church affairs, as well as in politics. His first office after his return was that of Judge of Probate, in which he served two years, from 1864. Then came an interval of a year and more in 1866 and 1867, spent with his mother in Providence, and employed in writing a life of President Wayland in collaboration with his brother.

Soon after his return to New Haven he was elected lieutenant governor of Connecticut, but after presiding over the senate with tact and success in the spring of 1869, Mr. and Mrs. Wayland again went abroad, spending that winter in Rome and the next in the south of England. By midsummer of 1871, they were again in New Haven and, with the exception of a single winter in the Hawaiian Islands, Mr. Wayland's subsequent life, somewhat varied and broken in upon hitherto, has been spent in charitable and philanthropic work, both scientific and practical, and in the service of the law department of Yale. The latter has been his life work.

The connection with the law school came about at the suggestion of President Woolsey, one of his last official acts. This school had been in a deplorable state. Its revival had been entrusted to three young lawyers, to whom Wayland was now added as professor of jurisprudence, 1872; he was made dean of the department the next year. But although the school had begun to feel the new life infused into it, in every material aspect it was sadly lacking. Its quarters were a pair of shabby rooms in the Leffingwell building. It had no library to speak of. An endowment was totally wanting. It had few students, small reputation, no assets in fact but the courage and faith and devotion of its professors. To build it up on the material side was the task to which the new dean set himself.

Hitherto, in a bald and statistical way, I have set forth the main facts of Professor Wayland's earlier life. But since 1876, as law student, instructor and professor, I have been in close association with him, and I claim the privilege of speaking of him as he impressed me.

This is the more permissible, for really his striking personality had much to do with his effectiveness. He was formed for dignified office by nature. Tall, rather portly, with fine features, a flowing beard, the art of address, tact, knowledge of men and wide acquaintance with the conspicuous figures of the period since the Civil War, he was altogether a man not to be withstood, a man who had his way. Add to this a ready pen, the gift of speech and of humor, uncommon sense, and a clear insight, and you have the dean as we younger men knew him. The great horse he rode, the delightful old-fashioned house he lived in, his whole environment suited and enhanced this personality.

The upbuilding of the department to which he gave himself was slow. It is only by a retrospect at considerable intervals that one sees how great it was. The first move of the school was to the spacious third story of the County Court House by grace of the commissioners. Then came the creation of a library and its endowment through the liberality of Governor English.

New professors were called, and the students grew, in numbers and in reputation. By gift of Mr. Morgan, the banker, of London, an endowment was begun and his son, Mr. J. P. Morgan, doubled it. Finally, in 1890, came the struggle to secure a permanent school buildiug, which has given us Hendrie Hall, Mr. J. W. Hendrie having contributed $65,000, the lot being furnished by the corporation.

In each of these advances Dean Wayland was the effective agent. As a beggar he was irresistible. You felt that it was more blessed to give than to decline. Meanwhile Professor Baldwin was carrying forward the school's standard of scholarship, pari passu, and owing to him a graduate department was added. The two men supplemented one another.

As an administrative officer, Professor Wayland is a master of detail. Discipline, correspondence, the purchase of furnishings, the decoration of the rooms, the hundred things which go to make an orderly academic life, for long all these fell to him alone. A system was created and we see the fruits of it.

Prizes for thesis writing and examination, encouragement of debate, lectures and lecture courses on topics germane but outside of the curriculum, the occasional hospitality shown by the school to students and friends, the relations of the school to the bar of the state; all these and many other matters, now almost a matter of course, bear the stamp of the dean's thought and effort in their origin.

Of course, in this laborious process of upbuilding, Professor Wayland had loyal and efficient aid from his colleagues. Equally of course there were often differences of opinion amongst them. But the one impression which these years of faculty discussion have made upon me is that of unity, of harmonious effort after a common end. Perhaps the ability to give and take, to differ without show of temper, is a characteristic of the legal profession. But I think in our own case we owed much to our presiding officer. His appreciation of our concord is well shown in a passage from a letter to the governing board of the school in reply to its resolutions upon his resignation, which I am permitted to quote.

"At this time, I recall with peculiar gratification the fact that during my entire intercourse with my associates — covering a period of more than thirty years — there has never been a single jarring note nor the faintest trace of friction, although there has been of course frequent difference of opinion."

In actual instruction Professor Wayland never took as active a part as some others, nor has he published extensively except in a fugitive way. I asked him why he had never gathered numerous scattered addresses and papers into book form now and then, and he said, "Oh, I have been too lazy." When I enumerate presently the offices in charitable and other organizatious which he has held, and the movements he has aided, his "laziness" will be still more apparent. But it is true that his life has been on somewhat different lines from that of his fellow Brunonian, Professor Fisher. The latter was first of all a scholar, a student of history, an original thinker in the domain of theology and Biblical criticism, and a voluminous writer on these varied subjects. Secondarily only did he turn to the work of administration. Wayland, on the other hand, as I have tried to show, was first of all an administrative officer and a man of affairs; in all his multifarious activities in and out of the Law School, one felt how strong he was on that side.

Of some of these activities I shall speak in a moment. But here to complete the account of his professional life, I should add that his first chair was that of Mercantile Law and Evidence; later he was made Professor of English Constitutional Law and in that capacity he has lectured on the history and scope of the English Constitution.

Towards his students he has ever shown himself a sympathetic friend, a just chief of department, an appreciative and appreciated teacher. Into his retirement the affection of all follows him.

This is a meagre record of Francis Wayland's professional career, but after all this has been only half his life. Let me place

PROFESSOR FRANCIS WAYLAND

together the impressive list of his offices and activities outside of his profession:

President of the Board of Connecticut State Prison Directors for fourteen years.

Chairman of the Executive Committee of the National Prison Congress for many years.

President of the Connecticut Prison Aid Association from 1875 until the present time.

President of the Organized Charities of New Haven for twenty-five years.

President of the American Social Science Association for three years, and

Chairman of its Department of Jurisprudence from 1876 to 1900.

On the Board of the Connecticut General Hospital; of the American Baptist Education Society; Vice-President American Baptist Missionary Union; President Board of Visitors at the U. S. Military Academy, 1874; Vice-President Board of

Visitors at the U. S. Naval Academy, 1880; Trustee Brown University, 1872-1888: Fellow Brown University, 1888 ——; a member of the New York University Club; of the New Haven Graduate Club; of the Connecticut Society of Colonial Wars; an LL. D. of Rochester, 1879, and of Brown, 1881; and doubtless other honors and offices have escaped notice.

On this other side of Mr. Wayland's life, the humanitarian side, the qualities which impress one are perseverance and common sense. He knew what he was after, knew that it was good and had the knack of putting it through.

The wood yard for the tramp evil, for instance, aad the abolition of indiscriminate out-door relief, add much to his vigorous advocacy. Into the reformation of prisoners' movement and the indeterminate sentence he went deeply, deeper than some of his friends could follow him.

In all these lines of charitable and sociological effort, he wrote and talked and worked. It was as hard to refuse him a paper as to refuse him money, and the consequence was that his causes prospered; he was a powerful friend.

A time of illness came in the midst of this most useful and active life, when shut in for many months he has borne confinement, pain and serious disease with a pluck and hopefulness which would not be denied. Yet always still the school and his other interests were on his mind and for them he has worked and planned. Now the clouds have lifted. Once more he bids fair to be equal to the round of daily duties. Not old in years, and younger still in heart, he may look confidently forward to the serenity and the usefulness of the years that are to come.

New Haven, April 16, 1903

BROWN MEN ON THE SUPREME BENCH

T H E connection between the Rhode Island supreme court and Brown University has for many years been intimate. It is doubtful if any other state has drawn so freely for its highest judges from any one college, and now that another Brown alumnus has been chosen to the bench, it seems an excellent time to put on record a statement of the close relationship of the college and the court.

Hon. Clarke H. Johnson of the class of 1877 has recently been elected associate justice of the supreme court of Rhode Island, to fill the vacancy caused by the retirement of Justice Horatio Rogers of the class of 1855.

Of the seven members at the present time four are graduates of Brown: Chief Justice John H. Stiness of the class of 1861, Associate Justices William W. Douglas of the class of 1861, John T. Blodgett of the class of 1880, and Clarke H. Johnson of the class of 1877.

Ever since the year 1827 the chief justiceship of Rhode Island has been held by a Brown graduate:

Hon. Samuel Eddy of the class of 1787 served from 1827 to 1835.

Hon. Job Durfee of the class of 1813 served from 1835 to 1847, in which year he died.

Hon. Richard W. Greene of the class of 1812 served from 1848 to 1854.

Hon. William R. Staples of the class of 1817 served from 1854 to 1856.

Hon. Samuel Ames of the class of 1823 served from 1856 to 1865, in which year he died.

Hon. Charles S. Bradley of the class of 1838 served from 1866 to 1868.

Hon. George A. Brayton of the class of 1824 served from 1868 to 1875.

Hon. Thomas Durfee of the class of 1846 served from 1875 to 1891.

Hon. Charles Matteson of the class of 1861 served from 1891 to 1900.

Hon. John H. Stiness of the class of 1861, the present chief justice, was appointed in 1900.

In the course of these seventy-five years a large number of Brown graduates have been members of the court. Levi Haile of the class of 1821 was an associate justice from 1835 to 1854; Alfred Bosworth of the class of 1835, was an associate justice from 1854 to 1862; J. Russell Bullock of the class of 1834 was a member of the court from 1862 to 1865; Walter S. Burges of the class of 1831 served from 1868 to 1881; George M. Carpenter of the class of 1864 was appointed in 1882 and served until 1885; Horatio Rogers of the class of 1855, who has recently retired, became a member of the court in 1891.

Prior to the appointment of Samuel Eddy to the chief justiceship in 1827, graduates of the college as follows, had occupied places on the bench: Samuel Randall of the class of 1804 was an associate justice from 1824 to 1833; Luke Drury of the class of 1813 was an associate justice from 1822 to 1824; Tristam Burges of the class 1796 was chief justice from 1817 to 1818; James. Burrill of the class of 1788 was chief justice from 1816 to 1817; and Thomas Arnold of the class of 1771 was chief justice from 1809 to 1810.

The founders of the college were men of public spirit, and in several instances, of marked legal ability as well. The first named trustee and first chancellor of the college, Hon. Stephen Hopkins, signer of the declaration of independence, first recipient of the honorary degree of doctor of laws from the college (the degree was given in 1784), was chief justice of Rhode Island in colonial days, from 1751 to 1756, and again from 1770 to 1774. The second chancellor of the college, Jabez Bowen, LL. D. (Dartmouth College, 1800), recipient of the honorary degree of master of arts at the first commencement in 1769, was an associate justice from 1776 to 1778, and was chief justice in 1781. David Howell, the first professor in the college, recipient of the honorary degree of master of arts in 1769 (he was a graduate of the College of New Jersey in the class of 1766), and of the degree of doctor of laws in 1793, was an associate justice from 1781 to 1782, and again from 1786 to 1787; Job Bennet of the original board of trustees was an associate justice from 1773 to 1776.

It should be noted that two professors in the college, Professor David Howell, LL. D., and Professor Tristam Burges, LL. D., have served on the supreme bench. Rev. Asa Messer, D. D., LL. D., of the class of 1790, president of the college from 1804 to 1826, was elected chief justice in June, 1818, but declined to serve. This is probably the only instance of a doctor of divinity having been elected to a post of administrative justice.

Sons of Brown have occupied places on the supreme benches of commonwealths other than Rhode Island. In Massachusetts the list includes:

Marcus Morton of the class of 1804, associate justice, 1825-1840.

Theron Metcalf of the class of 1805, associate justice, 1848-1865.

Charles Edward Forbes of the class of 1815, associate justice, 1848-49.

Benjamin F. Thomas of the class of 1830, associate justice, 1853-1859.

Marcus Morton of the class of 1838, associate justice, 1869-1882; chief justice, 1882-1890.

In New Hampshire, Reuben E. Walker of the class of 1875 was chosen associate justice in 1901.

In Vermont, Asa Aldis of the class of 1796 was chief justice in 1815.

In Maine, Ezekiel Whitman of the class of 1795 was chief justice, 1841-1848.

In Connecticut, Lafayette S. Foster of the class of 1828 was associate justice, 1870-1876.

In New York, William L. Marcy of the class of 1808 was associate justice, 1829-1831.

In Ohio, Franklin J. Dickman of the class of 1846 was associate justice, 1886-1894, and chief justice, 1894-1895.

In Michigan, Solomon Sibley of the class of 1794 was associate justice, 1824-1836.

In Georgia, John G. Polhill of the class of 1815 was associate justice.

In Kansas, Thomas Ewing of the class of 1856 was chief justice, 1861-62.

If there are any additions that should be made to this list the MONTHLY would be glad to hear of them and to record them as a matter of history.

THREE NEW COLLEGE GATES

THE CLASS OF 1872 GATE

WITHIN the near future there will be three new college gates at the university, one, near the corner of Prospect and Waterman streets, erected by the class of 1872 ; a second, built by the class of 1884 on Waterman street, adjoining Hope College, on the front campus, and the third, a memorial to John Nicholas Brown, '85, erected by Mrs. Brown and located on George street near the John Carter Brown Memorial Library.

The first of the side gates in the new college fence, given by the class of 1872, is nearly completed. It is situated on Prospect street, near the corner of Waterman street, and takes the place of the ancient passage through the old fence at the junction of the paths leading diagonally from Manning Hall and directly from Hope College. It was always, as now, the favorite passage-way to and from the boarding houses upon Waterman street. Nearly every surviving member of the class contributed to the cost of this gate. In the base of the north pier there has been placed a copper box hermetically sealed, which contains memorabilia of the class, illustrating its history while in college and the careers of its members since graduation. The list of the contents of this box may be interesting to other classes and is here inserted :

1. A list of the Class as matriculated in 1868.
2. An invitation to the Junior Exhibition, April 29, 1871.
   A Mock Programme of the Junior Exhibition.
3. A Typical Programme, Brown Glee Club, R. M. Elliott, '72, Conductor.
   A Programme, "Class of '72 Dramatic Entertainment."
6. An invitation to the "Exercises of Class Day," June 21, 1872.
7. A Programme of the "Class Day Exercises."
8. The Class Day "Oration and Poem."
9. The "Bill of Fare," "Class Supper," City Hotel.
10. The 104th Annual Commencement "Order of Exercises."
11. The Decennial Celebration, June 21, 1882, ' Menu."
12. The Fifteenth Anniversary, June 15, 1887, ' Menu."
13. Secretary's Circulars to Class, 1881, 1887, 1892, 1902.
14. Record of Class, 1872–1887.
15. Record of Class, 1872–1897, illustrated.
16. "Lays of Ancient Brown," resung at reunion, June 18, 1902.
17. Programme, Commencement Week, 1902.
18. General Circular of Fence Committee of Corporation, Feb., 1902.
19. Circular to Class Secretaries concerning Fence, March, 1902.

20. "Address Look" of Graduates of Brown University, December, 1901.
21. Brown Alumni Monthly, July, 1902.

The matriculation list containing fifty-eight names marks the earliest gathering of the members of the class on that June morning of 1868 when, with anxious parents, they presented themselves for examination for college. The list shows the full name, the age, the father's name if living, otherwise the mother's, the degree sought, A. B. or B. P., and the residence of each candidate.

The class did not come before the public until the invitations were sent out to its junior exhibition of April 29, 1871, which was travestied by that mixture of miscalled wit and asininity in the usual "mock programme." The impartial class historian, Frank Bartlett Greene, veraciously said of this class function: "'72 may well be proud of her junior exhibition, as it is the best that has taken place for many a year. The music of the college glee club was encored and deserves our notice as the singers owe their success in a great measure to the energetic efforts of their painstaking leader, Mr. Elliot, whose name will ever reflect honor on the class of '72. Moreover no other class furnishes so large a number of singers." On the strength of the last sentence a "typical programme" of the glee club was put in the box. At the concert in question, James May Duane, '72, assisted as cornet virtuoso. The programme of the "class of '72 dramatic

PRESIDENT ROBINSON
For Whom the Class of 1884 Will Name a Gate

entertainment," the first of a two nights' stand, which took place on the evening of the 26th of April, 1871, deserves preservation, for the show was given by certain "stagestruck juniors," animated by a desire to fill the treasury of the Brown nine. The class historian again avers that "the house was comparatively well filled," and

JOHN NICHOLAS BROWN GATE

that a most successful performance was "closed by a brilliant red light tableau of the university nine in their new uniforms. Thus an appropriate termination was given to the first night's performance;" and let us hope a substantial addition to the funds of the nine resulted. The happy final week of the class in college is outlined by the class day invitation programme of the "Exercises," the "oration and poem," the "bill of fare" of the class supper, and the order of exercises of the 104th annual commencement.

Succeeding items of the list have to do with successive reunions of the class, and with its thirty years of honorable and fairly successful struggle out in the world. Among other things the final items in the list give an outline of the fence movement in the circulars sent out for the information of graduates by the fence committee and its painstaking secretary. The last item, THE BROWN ALUMNI MONTHLY of July last, besides much interesting matter relating to commencement, contains the account of the last reunion of the class at the hospitable home on Benefit street of Robert Ives Gammell, where late on commencement evening the class gate became through generous and unanimous subscription an assured fact. Surely men of '72 at successive reunions may well sing with pride, as they gathers before this gate, in the words of the final stanza of that best of college hymns, as changed by the class historian above quoted :

"Oh! then as in memory backward we wander,
    And roam the long vista of past years adown,
On the scenes of our student life often we'll ponder,
    And smile, *as we think of our class* and Old Brown."

The contract for the 1884 gate has been awarded to Hoppin & Ely, who erected the Van Wickle gates and have in charge the construction of the sections of the new fence. They will begin work immediately and it is hoped that the gate will be completed by commencement time. The gate will be known as the Robinson gate, in memory of President Robinson. Though it is to be erected before next commencement, it will not be dedicated until June, 1904, when the class of 1884 will celebrate its twentieth anniversary. There is, furthermore, peculiar propriety in waiting until June, 1904, for the dedication of the gate in that it will then be exactly ten years since the death of President Robinson. He died on June 13, 1894, five years after retiring from the presidency. A committee consisting of Professor Henry B. Gardner, Frank H. Andrews, and M. J. Harson—the officers of the class—have charge of the erection of the gate.

A picture of the 1884 gate will probably appear in the next issue of the MONTHLY. Pictures of the other two are here given.

WOMEN SECRETARIES ORGANIZE

A MEETING that gives promise of producing important results took place, Wednesday afternoon, April 22, at the University Club, when the class secretaries of the Women's College gathered to talk over the formation of an association and to lunch as guests of the Brown Alumni Magazine Company.

As several of the class secretaries were too far from Providence to permit them to be present, other members of their classes were asked to attend and act for them *pro tempore*.

The meeting emphasized the desirability of having both the men's and women's classes elect secretaries whose homes are in Providence or not far distant.

Colonel Robert P. Brown, '71, treasurer of the magazine company, sat at the head of the luncheon table, which was beautifully decorated with roses and ferns. On his right was Dean Emery, on his left President Faunce. The secretaries and secretaries *pro tem.* present were : Mrs. Murdock, '95 ; Mrs. Frazee, '96 ; Mrs. Hood, '97 ; Miss Grant, '98 ; Miss Wilbur, '99 ; Miss Stark, 1900 ; Miss Burton, 1901 ; Miss Milliken, 1902 ; Miss Calef, 1903. In addition to these there were present Miss Stanton, registrar of the Women's College, and the editor, associate editor and business manager of the MONTHLY.

After the luncheon, Colonel Brown outlined the proposition for an association of class secretaries, reminding those present that a similar association of the secretaries of the men's classes had already been formed. He believed that a great work for Pembroke could be accomplished by such an organization and hoped that the young women present would decide to form one.

Miss Emery heartily approved the plan and so did President Faunce who followed her. Everybody present spoke briefly, and all were in favor of the suggestion. It was thereupon voted that an association be formed, and Dean Emery and Mrs. Murdock were appointed a committee to nominate officers. They reported as follows, and the report was unanimously accepted :

President, Mrs. Hood, '97. Secretary, Miss Stanton, '96. Executive Committee, The president, the secretary and Miss Burton, 1901.

The spirit of the meeting was one of great loyalty and enthusiasm. The general feeling was that a new era of usefulness for the class secretaries had opened, and that the Women's College would profit by the closer union of these graduate officials and the resulting closer contact of all the alumnæ.

RECENT DEBATING AT BROWN

FOR the last three or four years Brown has attained eminent success in the field of intercollegiate debating. In the three years previous to 1902–3 two victories were scored over Dartmouth, two over Boston University Law School, and one over Syracuse, while a single defeat by Dartmouth last year was registered against Brown. It was therefore a proud record which Brown set out to maintain this year, and well has she done so up to the time of writing.

The regular work of the year began with the annual sophomore-freshman debate on December 4, on the question " Resolved, That the system of direct primary nominations should be adopted in Rhode Island." The freshmen won after a spirited contest, in which both sides did themselves great credit.

The meeting with Dartmouth is always the chief event of the year in the debating line, and upon this years's event in particular depended to a great extent Brown's standing. Of the five debates which had occurred previous to this year Dartmouth had won three and Brown two ; a victory was therefore necessary to place Brown on an equal footing with her rival. The question was " Resolved, That Trades Unions should be compelled to incorporate," Brown taking the affirmative. The contest was held in Sayles Hall on February 26, and the Brown team—P. W. Gardner, '03, captain, E. L. McIntyre, '04' and A. B. West, '04—won a brilliant victory. At the close of the arguments proper the advantage seemed to lie with the men from Hanover, but in the rebuttals the Brown men completely turned the tables on their opponents, and the judges' decision met with universal approval.

The other varsity debate of the year is to be held at Syracuse on the second of May, over the question ".Resolved, That the present tendencies of Labor Unions are inimical to the industrial welfare of the United States." The Brown team is made up of P. R. Bakeman, '03, captain, G. B. Francis, Jr., '04, and W. E. Prince, '04' with C. H. Hull, '05' as alternate. The team has been training faithfully for three months, and with the excellent coaching it has received should bring back the hoped for victory.

Brown has always made a thorough knowledge of the question and a clear and logical development of the argument the chief aims in the training of her debating teams, and it is upon this solid foundation that she has always won, despite the fact that her opponents have usually been superior from an oratorical point of view. In real understanding of the fundamental points at issue and in ability to handle the arguments of their opponents the Brown men have been unsurpassed by any teams they have met.

The men comprising the second teams have labored as earnestly as the 'varsity debaters, and their efforts are thoroughly unselfish. No small share of credit for victories won is due to them ; and the training which they have received will be of inestimable value in future debating work.

THE
BROWN ALUMNI MONTHLY

Published for the graduates of Brown University

BY THE

Brown Alumni Magazine Co.

ROBERT P. BROWN, Treasurer, Providence, R. I.

Advisory Board

WILLIAM W. KEEN, '59, Philadelphia, Pa.
HENRY K. PORTER, '60, Pittsburg, Pa.
FRANCIS LAWTON, '69, New York, N. Y.
ROBERT P. BROWN, '71, Providence.
WILLIAM V. KELLEN, '72, Boston, Mass.
WILLIAM E. FOSTER, '73, Providence.
WINSLOW UPTON, '75, Providence.
ZECHARIAH CHAFEE, '80, Providence.
SAM WALTER FOSS, '82, Somerville, Mass.
GARDNER COLBY, '87, New York, N. Y.
WILLIAM R. DORMAN, '92, New York, N. Y.
GEORGE A. GASKILL, '98, Worcester, Mass.

HENRY R. PALMER, '90, Editor

JOSEPH N. ASHTON, '91, Associate Editor

THERON CLARK, '95, Business Manager

STEPHEN WATERMAN, '86, Advertising Manager

Address all communications to the BROWN ALUMNI MONTHLY, Brown University, except those relating to advertising, which should be sent to Mr. Waterman at 517 Angell street.
Subscription price, $1.00 a year. Single copies, Ten Cents. There is no issue during August and September.
Entered at the Providence post office as second-class matter.

MAY, 1903

THE ROBINSON GATE

It was surely a happy thought that led the class of 1884 to perpetuate in the gate it is about to erect at the university the name of Ezekiel Gilman Robinson. President Robinson was at the head of the college during all of Eighty-four's undergraduate course, and it is safe to say that there is not a member of the class who does not look back to that time with a feeling of respect and reverence for the serious and dignified gentleman whose personality impressed itself on students from their freshman days as a quality wholly in keeping with the best traditions of the college presidential office.

If any Brown alumnus retains among his undergraduate memories the recollection of an encounter with Dr. Robinson, either intellectual or personal, he cherishes it now as a valuable asset in his sum total of agreeable personal experiences. It may not have seemed funny, twenty years ago, to be interrupted in the building of an innocuous bonfire on the campus at midnight by the sudden appearance of a tall figure clad in sombre black and surmounted by the familiar presidential silk hat ; and caught by the collar maybe, or commanded in sonorous tones, " *Young man, go to your room !* " But the memory is highly prized after the lapse of years. It lends a reflected glory to the humblest Brunonian to have been associated, even in this temporarily unpleasant way, with President Robinson.

Brown men of a later day find it a common experience to hear Dr. Robinson praised by those who sat under him — praised as a distinguished executive and a strong preacher. He may not have been so well fitted by nature for the exercise of the multiform activities of the modern head of a great university, but he was the perfect type of the old-time college president. Upon that there will be substantial agreement. He had the gift of clear and pitiless logic, he was a profound student, he was the embodiment of scholastic dignity and propriety. Who can fail to remember now the sturdy straightening of his tall form in chapel, the proud attitude of lofty head and well-poised shoulders, the delicious mingling of austere words with the twinkle of appreciative wit beneath the snowy eyebrows ! We may not all have loved him then, but we respected him. He was genuine, all through, except so far as some of his austerity may have been assumed in self-defence against an inconvenient kindliness of heart. But it is not too much to say that we all love his memory — our memory of him as he comes back to us, erect behind the faded green fringe of the chapel pulpit, or leaning far forward in an earnest sermon, or pursuing his unbending way across the campus, seal and symbol of everything worth knowing or being in the realm of the intellectual life.

So it is that we are all glad — we older graduates — to have the class of 1884 erect its handsome new gate as a memorial to President Robinson and to realize that it will be " the Robinson gate " so long as it swings on its metal hinges and so long as its posts of brick and stone endure.

STONE COLLEGE BUILDINGS

Brick is an excellent material for college buildings, but stone has a dignity that no other material possesses. Oxford and Cambridge would lose a great deal in ponderous charm if High and Trumpington streets were lined with cloistered colleges of red or yellow brick, however old and dingy. One longs, indeed, when he sees these ancient stone quadrangles, flaked and grim, for something of the tidiness and convenience of the modern American college hall (unless he is a hopeless sentimentalist), but the ensemble is certainly finer than it would be if brick and brick alone had been used.

Here at Brown we have our " old brick row " — at least one of the stuccoed buildings is brick — but on the farther side of the middle campus a new stone row is in process of evolution. First Sayles Hall was built, a little more than twenty years ago, of a fine red granite with brownstone trimmings. Next Wilson Hall was erected, in 1890, immediately south of Sayles, the material being an olive sandstone which, in the fine architectural lines of the building, is peculiarly attractive to the eye. Now the John Carter Brown library is fast rising next south of Wilson, and in a few weeks its white marble will present an effective contrast to the color scheme of its two stone neighbors.

ADVANTAGES OF BROWN

Every college has its own peculiar advantages, as well as its disadvantages. At this season, when the academic year is drawing to a close and many young men in preparatory schools are undecided as to which college they will choose, it may be well to put forward modestly a few of the advantages of Brown.

1. It is a city college, affording students who have to work their way through, in whole or in part, infinitely greater opportunities than they would enjoy in a small town.

2. This same fact of Brown's city location inures to the great advantage of those other students who are not dependent on their own resources to carry them through and who desire the social opportunities that life in a small town will not bring.

3. At the same time, Providence, a city of less than 200,000 people, is not large enough to obscure the university, as Columbia University, the College of the City of New York and New York University are obscured by their location in the metropolis. Brown is set on a hill two hundred feet above the centre of the city, with a large and pleasant campus, and only a mile away is the Seekonk river, wooded on either shore and affording the best of opportunities for aquatic sports. A little farther on is the beautiful Ten Mile river, than which there is no more charming sylvan stream in New England. Tennis, golf, baseball — all the outdoor sports that increase the attractiveness of country life — are found at Brown, and in addition every desirable intellectual element of city life like Kneisel concerts, lectures by men of national reputation and the best dramatic performances.

4. Brown is a growing university. It is only beginning its expansion, material and intellectual. At the present time there are in course of erection upon the campus the Bajnotti clock tower, the John Carter Brown Memorial Library, the mechanical engineering building, Rockefeller Hall for social and religious purposes, and a new dormitory. A new administration building was built a few months ago and the Hoyt swimming pool has been open only a few weeks.

TOPICS OF THE MONTH

ROCKEFELLER HALL has not yet begun to rise above the surface of the middle campus, but the excavation for the basement is nearly completed. The John Carter Brown Library shows its white walls for ten or twelve feet above ground and gives promise of being a thing of beauty and a joy forever. The exterior of the engineering building on Lincoln Field is finished and a wooden railing around the roof gives it an improved appearance. The interior walls of the new dormitory on Thayer street are rapidly rising, but the exterior walls are not as yet begun. The foundation for the Bajnotti clock tower is ready and the beautiful structure will be well on toward completion in another month or so. The campus is a busy place, these spring days, with the workmen on the several new structures scattered about and the students, as usual when the first warm days come, grouped around in large numbers. There are worse ways to spend a leisure hour than to sit on a pile of lumber on the campus some bright May morning and watch the workmen at their labors. There is plenty of life and bustle in the scene, and the imaginative Brown man can ponder pleasantly on what all this material growth means and what the future expansion of the university is destined to be.

ૐ

Dr. Parker   Dr. Fred E. Parker has
Leaves Brown   resigned the directorship of physical culture in the university, which he has held for the past twelve years, to take charge of a newly established health institute at Warwick, R. I. Dr. Parker was the first director of physical culture at Brown, and his services have been eminently successful. Under his direction compulsory gymnasium work has been regularly and profitably carried on by all four classes. Several New England colleges require gymnasium work, but Brown alone requires it for the entire undergraduate period. Despite this and the fact that the student body outgrew the accommodations of the gymnasium several years ago, he has prosecuted the work with uniform success. He has, furthermore,

always taken a lively interest in athletics at Brown and has devoted much time and effort to promote them.

Dr. Parker was graduated at Bowdoin College in 1891. Throughout his college course he held the championship in heavyweight boxing and wrestling, and during his junior and senior years was captain and stroke of the eight-oared crew. In the summers of 1891, 1892 and 1893 he was a student of physical culture in the Harvard Summer School. In the summers of 1896, 1897 and 1898, and during the academic year of 1898–99, he studied medicine at the Dartmouth Medical School, from which he received the degree of doctor of medicine in March, 1899.

Last year he was elected vice-president of the National College Gymnasium Directors' Society.

ૐ

Absence Granted   Three members of
for the Year 1903-4   the Brown faculty, Professor Everett of the department of philosophy, Professor Greene of the department of Latin, and Mr. Morse of the department of Romance languages, will spend the next academic year in study abroad.

Professor Everett will take his sabbatical year, "as a matter of principle," to use his own words. He believes that it is highly desirable for the university that its professors should occasionally escape the ruts of academic routine, and, more especially, that they should have periods in which to devote themselves to study and writing with a degree of concentration altogether impossible during the pressure of active work. Like many other Brown professors he has had not a few demands upon his time for services outside of the university lecture room, and is looking forward to next year with the hope of devoting himself exclusively to his chosen studies. Professor Everett has already spent a year in study at two of the leading German universities, Berlin and Strassburg, and is therefore familiar with German university methods. It is not his purpose to attend lectures during his year of absence, but to devote himself chiefly to writing. His itinerary is not definitely fixed. After spending the summer in Switzerland he will probably go to Germany and locate in some university town which offers good library facilities. In the spring he hopes to go to Italy.

Professor Greene will sail for Marseilles in July and will spend the month of August in Provence visiting the Roman ruins there. He will spend September at Siena and in October will visit the cities of Etruria and the Italian towns in the vicinity of Rome. By the end of October he will take up his residence in Rome for the winter. During the spring he will visit Greece, and possibly Northern Africa.

Mr. Morse will divide his period of residence abroad between Italy and France. He will spend the summer in Italy and the winter in Paris. In Italy he will study at Siena and at Paris will pursue courses in Old French and Provençal at the university. On his way to Paris he will visit parts of Northern Italy, Provence and Dauphiny. At Easter time he will make a trip to Italy, returning to Paris to complete the academic year at the university there. The following summer will be spent in Southern France.

*

Faculty Appointments for 1903-04 In the department of comparative anatomy Michael X. Sullivan, A. M., will be an instructor in physiology, and will conduct the courses of Professor Tower, who has resigned his position at Brown to accept a position in the American Museum of Natural History in New York. Mr. Sullivan received the degree of bachelor of arts in Harvard University in 1899 and the degree of master of arts in Brown University in 1902. He is at present a candidate for the degree of doctor of philosophy at Brown.

During Professor Everett's absence abroad his courses in philosophy will be conducted by Stephen S. Colvin, Ph. D., assistant professor of philosophy in the University of Illinois. Dr. Colvin was graduated at Brown in 1891. For three years subseqent to his graduation he remained at the university as an instructor in English. He then studied abroad and obtained the doctorate in philosophy in the University of Strassburg in 1897. From 1897 to 1901, when he was appointed to his present position in the University of Illinois, he was teacher of English in the Worcester High School.

In the department of Latin Mr. Ernest T. Paine of the class of 1901 will have charge of Professor Greene's courses. Mr. Paine has been giving several of these courses this year while Professor Greene has been conducting the courses ordinarily given by Professor A. G. Harkness, who is on leave of absence and is serving as the director of the American School of Classical Studies in Rome for the present academic year.

*

The Dickerman Collection The university library has received from the estate of the Rev. Lysander Dickerman, D. D., of the class of 1851, the library of that distinguished Egyptologist, which comprises about 1,200 volumes. The collection represents the general library of a scholar, but is particularly strong in books pertaining to Egyptian and Biblical archæology. Among the important Oriental works are Binion's Ancient Egypt, in two large folio volumes; the proceedings of the Society of Biblical Archæology, in 20 volumes; Brugsch's Hieroglyphisches Woerterbuch in 7 volumes, his Recueil de Monuments Egyptiens, in 2 volumes, besides other works by the same scholar; the Book of the Dead, translated by Davis; Duemischen's Inschriften, in 3 volumes, and his Photographische Resultate; the Memoirs of the Egypt Exploration Fund, in 8 volumes; the publication of the American Oriental Society, in 14 volumes; and Maspero's Historie Ancienne, in 3 volumes. Included in the gift are Dr. Dickerman's numerous unpublished notes on Egyptology and the manuscripts of his lectures. Through the generosity of Mrs. Dickerman her husband's library is accompanied by his collection of lantern-slides, which is, perhaps, the most complete in America. It consists of 524 slides, some of them beautifully colored.

This valuable collection of books and slides will at once be an important aid as well as a powerful stimulus to Egyptian and Semitic studies at Brown.

*

Enlargement of the Harris Collection The Harris Collection of American Poetry came into the possession of the university in 1884 as a bequest from the Hon. Henry B. Anthony of the class of 1833. The collection numbered about 6,000 volumes and remained without addition, except for a few volumes presented by authors, until 1898, when Samuel C. Eastman, Esq., of the class of 1857 began to make frequent contributions toward its development. Up to the present time his gifts have amounted to more than a thousand volumes.

In March of the present year the librarian received from Mr. Eastman a letter in which he stated that, since he no longer found frequent opportunities to purchase books for the Harris Collection, he wished to establish a fund, the income of which should be used for that purpose. His letter was accompanied by a four per cent. bond for $1,000, and the request was added that the books so purchased should bear a plate in memory of Albert G. Greene of the class of 1820, the original founder of the collection. Mr. Eastman is a son-in-law of Judge Greene, and was familiar with the collection before it came into the possession of C. Fiske Harris, from whose estate it was purchased by Senator Anthony. He was also connected with the university library as assistant librarian during his first year after graduation.

The gift from Mr. Eastman recalls that of the same amount from Chancellor Goddard in 1900 for the purchase of rare books for the Harris Collection at the McKee Sale in New York. Another recent source of substantial increase to the collection has been the $1,500 derived from the sale of duplicates in 1901. But, in spite of these additions, there still remains, to employ the language of Mr. Edmund Clarence Stedman in his *Victorian Anthology*, "an enviable opportunity for the friends of this notable collection to place it beyond rivalry by filling in many of its gaps," and, we may add, by making still more ample provision for its future.

***

A Book of Brown Stories   A book of short stories about Brown life, written by Frederick William Jones, ex-'96, a member of the Providence Journal staff, will be brought out early in May. It will be called "A Year at Brown."

Stories of this kind have been written about almost all the larger colleges, but thus far Brown has been neglected. One reason for this neglect is undoubtedly due to the fact that there are not a sufficient number of Brown alumni to make a book solely devoted to their Alma Mater assuredly profitable to the publisher. Snow & Farnham of Providence, who will print the Brown stories, have undertaken the work, however, with the thought of turning out a book that will be of considerable interest to the people of Rhode Island generally and to Brown men everywhere. They realize that it is a book with a limited field, but they are confident that it will thoroughly cover that field and that everyone interested in the college will wish to read it. Only a limited number of copies will be issued.

The stories are all fictitious, but the pictures of college life around which they are written are familiar to all Brown men. The time is in the early '90s, in the days of President Andrews. The background used for the tales is made up of important occasions in the college year. The first story deals with the return to college in the fall, the reunion of old friends and a mild form of hazing; the second with a fraternity "rushing" meeting; the third with a "big" football game; the fourth with a gym. ball; the fifth with Class day and the sixth with commencement. There are two other stories in the book, but they are not associated with "red letter" days at Brown.

Sydney R. Burleigh, the well-known Providence artist, is the illustrator.

The price will be $1.50 and subscriptions can be sent at any time to the publishers.

***

University Club in a Vermont Town   In the little town of Proctor, Vermont, there is an unusually large number of college men. For some time there was talk of forming a university club. On the evening of October 17, 1902, there was held a meeting at the home of G. W. C. Hill, Brown, '92. Twenty-three men sat down to supper. Old college songs and other usual accompaniments of such an occasion made it a most enjoyable time. When supper was over there were remarks by various ones, in which much interest was expressed in the proposed scheme, and an organization was effected. Mr. Hill was made president and W. D. Abbott, Dartmouth, '93, vice president. There were twenty-two charter members, representing ten different colleges, both American and European.

The club then listened to a most interesting talk by Professor Theodore Henckels of Middlebury College on " A Comparison of German and American Methods of Education." Thus began the University Club of Proctor, Vt., the second and the largest club in the state.

At a recent banquet, February 13, tendered the club by one of its members, Hon. F. D. Proctor, Amherst, '82, there were thirty present, and the membership had grown to thirty-four, representing fifteen colleges. Of this number is Hon. Redfield Proctor, senior senator from Vermont.

Reside the meetings for social and literary purposes there is the purpose of arousing and fostering a college sentiment amongst the young people of the high school. And there are evidences that such an influence is already at work.

The University Club of Proctor has no building or rooms. They are not necessary. But it has in abundant measure that spirit that characterizes the fine brotherhood of college men, and it is doing something practical to keep alive in its members loyalty to the university ideal and to their several alma maters.

&

Faculty Notes Mr. J. Franklin Collins has recently published a fifteen-page pamphlet which is now being used by students in Botany 3 as a descriptive guide in the systematic field and laboratory work which constitutes a part of that course.

Professor William MacDonald, who is president of the New England History Teachers' Association for the present year, presided at the spring meeting of the association, which was held at the Girls' Latin School, Boston, April 18.

CHRONICLE OF THE CAMPUS

JUNIOR week has been the chief undergraduate event of the month at the college. An account of this interesting annual event is printed elsewhere in this issue. The university nine returned early in the month from the South, after a pleasant trip which resulted in some victories and some defeats ; and celebrated the return by winning twice from the Providence league team. The campus is much torn up with the excavations for the clock tower, Rockefeller Hall, the John Carter Brown library, the new engineering building and the Thayer street dormitory. On the night of April 11 more than 200 undergraduates, alumni and " sub-freshmen " dined at the gymnasium and made merry with speeches and songs. This was the second annual " Brown banquet."

Baseball Season to Date

BROWN, 4 ; NORTH CAROLINA, 1

The university nine and substitutes left Providence by steamer for Norfolk, Va., March 24. Almost the entire party was seasick, but when the first game of the southern series was played at Chapel Hill, N. C., against the University of North Carolina, on March 27, it resulted in a victory for Brown, 4 to 1. The weather was perfect and 1,000 people witnessed the game.

For five innings neither side could score and it looked as if the game would be a pitchers' battle to the finish. But in the sixth, with one out, Gray of Brown bunted safely, took second on a passed ball and scored on Metcalf's slashing drive to right field. Carolina evened matters in the same innings by bunching a single and double, helped along by

an excusable passed ball by Clark. In the eighth, however, Brown opened up by bunching three hits, which, coupled with a few timely errors, sent three runs across the plate. For the remainder of the game the Southerners cheered valiantly for their team, but it was no use, and the ninth inning ended with the score of 4 to 1 in favor of Brown.

Lynch was easily the star of the game, allowing but three safe hits and getting two fine drives himself, one for a single and the other for two bases. The home team made three hits and four errors.

The fielding of the entire Brown team was exceptionally good, but one error being credited to them, and that on a hard drive to Penley.

BROWN, 7 ; NORTH CAROLINA, 12

At Greensboro, N. C., on March 28, North Carolina reversed the Brown victory of the day before. Whiting pitched most of the game for Brown.

BROWN, 1 ; GEORGETOWN, 4

Wet grounds prevented the proposed meeting of Brown and the University of Virginia, but the northern visitors explored Charlottesville and were highly pleased with the classic architecture and picturesque situation of the institution founded by Thomas Jefferson.

At Washington, D. C., April 1, Georgetown beat Brown 4 to 1. The weather was ideal and 500 people witnessed the contest. Georgetown went to bat first, but was retired in quick order, as was Brown in her half. In the second, however, the home team started the ball rolling by scoring one on an error by Pattee, a long fly to the outfield and a two-base hit by Keane. Again in the sixth a passed ball by Clark, followed by a hit, gave them another.

Brown did nothing until the seventh, when Penley scored from second on a slashing drive by Pattee over second base. Previous to this, the visitors had two opportunities with three men on bases to win out; but the required hit was not forthcoming. In the third inning Hatch reached first on an error of the centre fielder, and went to third on Pattee's bunt. Morgan fumbled Gray's grounder, filling the bases. With three men on bases and one out, Clark came to the bat and hit directly in front of the plate, making an easy double play possible.

Georgetown scored twice in the eighth on a line drive to left field for two bases with the bases full. Metcalf made a fine try for the hit, but only succeeded in blocking it and holding the batter at second.

The features of the game were the pitching of Hatch and Drill and the fielding of Pattee. Brown's batting was weak, as was also that of Georgetown, but the latter's was very timely, the entire four runs being driven in by work at the bat.

BROWN, 9; COLUMBIAN, 5

On April 2, at Washington, Brown defeated Columbian University, 9 to 5, though the fielding of our men was poorer than on the day before.

Brown went to bat first and scored three times on hits by Gray, Clifford and Lynch, aided by two timely errors. These were duplicated in the third when Lynch slammed the ball over the left field fence for a homer, bringing in two men ahead of him. Again in the sixth two more added, and in the eighth Pattee scored the last run by stealing second and scoring on Gray's two bagger to left.

Whiting started in to do the twirling for Brown and before he could get steadied down three runs came across the plate. In the second the Northerners had a comedy of errors and presented their opponents with two more runs, bringing their total to five. For the remainder of the game the men from the capital were not dangerous and Lynch, who went in the box the last inning, quickly struck out the first three men to face him.

The features of the game were the hitting of Gray and Lynch, the latter's home run drive being the longest ever made on the held.

Brown made 13 hits and 7 errors; Columbian, 3 hits and 6 errors.

BROWN, 2; PHILADELPHIA AMERICAN, 9

Lynch pitched a good game, April 3, against the Philadelphias, champions of last year's American League, but the professionals won, 9 to 2. Brown made 4 hits and 4 errors, Philadelphia 8 hits and 2 errors.

Rain prevented the Brown-Fordham game, April 4.

BROWN, 5; PROVIDENCE, 2

For the first time in several years Brown beat the Providence team of the Eastern League at Adelaide Park April 11. Lynch pitched and the professionals made only six hits off his delivery. The score by innings:

										r.	h.	e.
Brown	0	0	2	0	0	0	3	0	0—5	7	2
Providence	0	0	2	0	0	0	0	0	0—2	6	10

BROWN, 4; PROVIDENCE, 3

Brown won the second game with the Providence leaguers at Adelaide Park April 18. Hatch pitched

effectively and Lynch won the game in the ninth inning when the score was tied by a home-run drive over the centrefield fence. The score by innings:

										r.	h.	e.
Brown	1	0	2	0	0	0	0	0	1—4	7	6
Providence	2	0	0	0	0	1	0	0	0—3	4	2

BROWN 3; WESLEYAN, 0

The feature of Brown's defeat of Wesleyan at Adelaide Park, April 22, was Hatch's pitching. With three men on bases and one out he extricated himself from a bad hole in the fifth by striking out the last two men. The score:

										r.	h.	e.
Brown	0	0	1	0	0	2	0	0	x—3	5	4
Wesleyan	0	0	0	0	0	0	0	0	0—0	4	3

BROWN, 2; PRINCETON, 0

Princeton's strong team was shut out by Brown at Adelaide Park April 25. Lynch allowed the visitors only three hits, and Stearns of Princeton was equally parsimonious with the Brown batters. A wild throw by McClave, the Princeton catcher, netted Brown two runs, the only ones scored by either side during the game. Brown's play was errorless. By innings:

										r.	h.	e.
Brown	0	0	2	0	0	0	0	0	0—2	3	0
Princeton	0	0	0	0	0	0	0	0	0—0	3	2

BROWN, 3; YALE, 9

Brown went to pieces in the fourth inning at New Haven, April 30, after holding the lead 2 to 0. MacKinney, substitute leftfielder, dropped an easy fly and the errors began to accumulate. Eight Yale runs came in before the third man was put out, the umpire apparently "roasting" the Brown players at every opportunity. Let us hope he was honest. Outside of this inning Brown played better than Yale and Hatch pitched well. Westcott pitched for Yale. The crowd was the largest of the season at New Haven.

										r.	h.	e.
Brown	0	1	1	0	0	0	0	0	1—3	8	4
Yale	0	0	0	8	0	0	1	0	0—9	12	3

THE RECORD TO DATE

Brown,	4	North Carolina,	1
"	7	" "	12
"	1	Georgetown,	4
"	9	Columbian,	5
"	2	Philadelphia,	9
"	5	Providence,	2
"	4	Providence,	3
"	6	Williams,	2
"	3	Wesleyan,	0
"	2	Princeton,	0
"	3	Yale,	9

GAMES YET TO BE PLAYED

May	9.	Yale, at Andrews Field.
	12.	Pennsylvania, at Philadelphia.
	13.	Princeton, at Princeton.
	16.	Dartmouth, at Andrews Field.
	20.	Andover, at " "
	23.	Yale, at ' "
	27.	Dartmouth, at Hanover.
	30.	Georgetown, at Andrews Field.
June	3.	Harvard, at " "

June 6. Williams, at Andrews Field.
     10. Pennsylvania, at "   "
     12. Pennsylvania, at "   "
     15. Amherst, at Amherst.
     17. Lafayette, at Andrews Field.

Hicks Prize Debate

A preliminary contest for the Hicks prize debate held on will be May 6, at 8 o'clock, in Manning Hall. Each speaker will be allowed to speak ten minutes. Contestants must submit their names to Professor Huntington on or before Monday, May 4, at noon.

At this preliminary contest four speakers for the final contest will be chosen by a committee appointed by the president of the university, and consisting of Professors Bronson, Huntington and Dealey.

The final contest will occur on Thursday evening, June 11, at 8 o'clock, in Manning Hall. Twelve minutes will be allowed each speaker for his first speech and five minutes for his rebuttal. The committee of award will consist of five members, two chosen by the president of the university, two by a majority of the contestants, and one by the faculty.

The question for the preliminary contest is the following : Resolved, That article fifth of the constitution of the United States should be so changed as to allow amendments to be ratified by a majority instead of three-fourths of the several states.

Governor Garvin will preside.

Junior Week

The several functions of Junior week were successfully carried out on April 20 and the days immediately succeeding. They included a concert by the musical clubs at Sayles Hall and an informal dance in the gymnasium afterwards, a lecture by Rev. R. H. Conwell of Philadelphia, several fraternity teas, a presentation of the curtain-raiser "Prexy's Proxy" and the farce "The Snowball" by the Sock and Buskin Society at the Providence Opera House, a Brown-Wesleyan ball game at Adelaide Park, and the annual junior promenade at Sayles Hall. The Opera House held a large and brilliant audience at the Sock and Buskin performance, and the best of college feeling prevailed. Confetti was showered from the gallery, and a specially uproariously greeting was given to the students who took the part of fair damsels on the stage. The "junior prom." was a charming society event, with music by Clarke's Providence Orchestra. Sayles Hall was decked with evergreen boughs and laurel and presented a beautiful sight.

Carpenter Speaking Contest

The trials for the Carpenter prize speaking contest, April 8, brought out more contestants than have reported at any other time in the last three years. The judges of the trials were Professor Crosby, Mr. Latham and Mr. Guild, of the English department. The seven men following were chosen :

L. W. Cronkhite, C. H. Hull, C. H. Kingman, W. L. Pratt, E. M. Wilson, G. W. Woodin, C. C. Zaslavsky. The contest will take place at the First Baptist Church, June 15.

Tennis at Brown

Brown is a member of the New England Intercollegiate Tennis Association, and now leads in the number of points won toward the permanent possession of the cup offered the college first winning eight points. Brown has three points toward this, which is double the number held by the nearest opponent. The intercollegiate meet will be held at Longwood, Mass., on May 25.

Negotiations with Amherst for a dual tournament at some date prior to the Longwood meet are now under way, and a round robin tournament is to be held to determine Brown's representatives at these contests.

Various Items

Fourteen additional sections of the new fence have arrived and are being erected.

The seniors appeared for the first time in their caps and gowns at chapel, March 3. They marched to Sayles Hall in a body and were seated in the front of the hall during chapel exercises.

The *Brown Daily Herald* says that the April *Brunonian* is too serious in tone and declares that the purpose of the magazine is "to amuse and entertain." How does it know?

In Sayles Hall the paintings are covered with white cloths to protect them during the repairs to the balcony necessitated by the putting in of the new organ.

A provisional band has been formed with 21 members.

There is now a Brown golf team, which expects to enter one or more intercollegiate contests before the summer vacation.

A Columbia-Brown whist tournament opens at Providence May 9.

The new turf diamond at Andrews Field is at last in readiness, and the new cinder track is approaching completion.

The bowling team has finished the season with third honors in the league. The average of play was higher than ever before.

Homer W. Guernsey, a brother of a former Brown baseball player and of ex-Captain Guernsey of the Yale nine, has been elected captain of the Brown freshman team. He comes from Riverview Academy, Poughkeepsie, N. Y.

Pembroke beat Radcliffe College at basketball a few days ago.

Pembroke's dramatic society, the Komians, give "Pygmalion and Galatea" May 2. Dancing will follow the play.

BRUNONIANS FAR AND NEAR

1828 and 1846

The *Boston Herald* recently contained the following editorial comment:

"Apropos of the resignation of Dean Francis Wayland (Brown, '46,) of the Yale law school, it is remarked of him that in addition to his other accomplishments he has been a remarkably successful money getter for that institution. It was Dean Wayland who invited the late Lafayette Foster (Brown, '28,) to lecture before the law school, and the impoverished condition of the institution was fully explained to Mr. Foster. A few weeks later Mr. Foster informed Dean Wayland that he would remember the law school in his will, and when Mr. Foster died it was found that his will provided that his estate should go to the school upon the death of his widow. Whenever Mrs. Foster and Dean Wayland met afterward Mrs. Foster would say: "You see, I am still alive." "I see you are," the dean would reply, "but peace to your ashes." Mrs. Foster died a few months ago, and the Yale law school now comes into full possession of the estate."

Mr. Foster represented his native state, Connecticut, in both branches of congress. He was a member of the house of representatives, 1839-41, 1846-48, 1854-55, and of the senate from 1855 to 1867. Upon the accession of Andrew Johnson to the presidency in 1865 Mr. Foster became president pro tempore of the senate and served in that capacity during the remainder of the thirty-ninth congress.

Mr. Foster received the honorary degree of doctor of laws from Brown in 1851. By his will he gave to his Alma Mater a fund for the establishment of a premium for excellence in Greek studies. In accordance with the terms of the donor's will, the income of this fund is to be "annually paid to that scholar of the institution who passes the best examination in the Greek language, the examination to be made in the first, third and twenty-fourth books of Homer's Iliad or in the Oration on the Crown by Demosthenes."

1839

Charles C. Burnett died at his home in West Springfield, Mass., April 8, at the age of eighty nine. He was born in Worcester, October 16, 1813. Soon after his graduation at Brown he took charge of the Connecticut Literary Institution at Suffield. Later, in the sixties, he bought the English and Classical Institute of Springfield and spent there many of the best years of his life. He also taught for a time in Worcester Academy. Mr. Burnett was one of the charter members of the Brown chapter of the Delta Phi fraternity.

1840

Rev. Obil Windsor Briggs, the oldest member of the Brown Club of California, died in San Francisco, Cal., November 11, 1902. He was born at Waterville, Maine, May 28, 1820.

He came of good New England stock. His great grandfather was Deacon George Briggs of Norton, Mass. His grandfather, Rev. Joel Briggs, served in the Colonial Army, and was an honorary graduate of Brown; he received the degree of master of arts as an honorary degree at commencement, 1795.

His father, Rev. Avery Briggs, was graduated at Brown in the class of 1816, and was a professor in Waterville College, now Colby College, from 1822 to 1828.

After graduating at Brown in 1840, Obil W. Briggs studied law for a time; deciding, however, to enter the ministry, he entered Newton Theological Seminary, from which he was graduated in 1844.

His first pastorate was at the Eutaw Place Baptist Church, Baltimore, where he succeeded the Rev. Dr. Fuller. His second settlement was at Alexandria, Va. Later he was called to the First Baptist Church, Brooklyn, N. Y. On the breaking out of the Civil War he accepted the chaplaincy of the 9th Illinois Cavalry, and served until compelled by disability to resign.

He went to California in 1863, where for two years he acted as agent for the Freedman's Bureau. Owing to impaired health he never accepted a settled pastorate. During the last twelve years of his life he held a position in the Federal Court at San Francisco, where he was loved and respected by all with whom he came in contact.

Mr. Briggs was twice married; in 1844 he married Miss Julia Scribner of Baltimore, who died in 1850; and in 1858 he married Mrs. Mary S. Champney.

He died after a short illness, at the age of eighty-two years, five months, and eleven days, leaving a widow and three daughters.

1852

Rev. George Dana Boardman, D. D., LL. D., of Philadelphia, died at Atlantic City, N. J., April 28. An extended report of his notable career will be printed in these pages next month.

1864

A meeting of the incorporators of the Ratcliffe Hicks Industrial and Educational Institute was held in Bridgeport, Conn., April 14. A board of trustees was elected and an organization effected. The proposed institute, which was incorporated by the last Connecticut general assembly, will be located in the town of Tolland. Hon. Ratcliffe Hicks, Brown, '64, who is a native of that Connecticut country town, proposes to expend a large fund for the development of the institution. He says: "It is my idea to plan this school after the more successful manual schools in the United States and to fit every boy and girl for some useful, remunerative occupation or trade, such as engineering, surveying, architecture, bookkeeping, typewriting, and so on. In this town of Tolland I hope to found an institution to which the youth of both sexes without any religious distinctions may be invited to come and fit themselves for the arduous struggles and the varied responsibilities of life."

The charter stipulates that the board of trustees shall consist of not less than ten nor more than twenty members. It forbids the withholding of the privileges of the school from any person on account of religious opinions. It provides that in case more qualified persons than can be accommodated apply for admission to the institution, selection of candidates shall be made in this order: First, from the town of Tolland; second, from Tolland County; third, from the State of Connecticut; and lastly, from the United States.

A sketch of Mr. Hicks and of his plans for the institute appeared in the MONTHLY some time ago.

1865

Mr. and Mrs. J. Mitchell Clark of New York are erecting at Newport a notable Italian house. It is situated three miles from the centre of the city and about two miles from the last row of fine houses along the Cliff walk. It has been built with the idea of making it seem ancient from the beginning. The stone is almost black and the mortar has been darkened to match it, so that the structure looks like a mediæval castle taken bodily from its original surroundings and set down close to the cottage district of a modern American summer resort. The name of the estate is "Gray Craig." The rock used in the construction of the new house crops out of the soil everywhere on the farm and is admirably adapted to the purpose.

Last April the work began, and some time this spring it will be completed. Every step taken has either been directed by Mr. and Mrs. Clark or followed by them with the keenest interest. They have spent many hours each day for months suggesting original ideas or listening to suggestions from the workers. The masons were especially proud of their task, and after they had been taught how to lay the mortar to give the building an appearance of age they began to devise means by which they could add half a century or more of age to the looks of the walls and towers. Mrs. Clark is herself an artist, and the results of her skill are shown in many ways about "Gray Craig." The Italian gardens back of the castle have been her especial field.

In their travels through Europe and particularly through Italy, Mr. and Mrs. Clark collected many beautiful pieces of statuary and entablature, which they are now using to adorn the house and its surroundings. Bas-reliefs and medallions taken from the catacombs of Rome have been cemented into the walls of the building here and there. The old keystones in the Gothic arches at the base of the sixty-five foot tower under which the main entrauce to the castle is gained were also imported from Italy.

Ancient as the castle will be in looks, some of the accessories will be most modern, both in appearance and in reality. They will be kept out of sight, however, as much as possible, for, while they may be convenient and comfortable, even indispensable, they belong to the twentieth century, and so do not harmonize with a castle of the Middle Ages. There will be no stables. Only automobiles will be used, and the house for them in the courtyard is concealed behind a mediæval lookout.

Mr. Clark, is a son of Bishop Thomas M Clark of Rhode Island.

1870

Professor W. H. Munro lectured, April 15, on "The State of Society in France Before the Revolution" at the monthly smoker of the Unity Club of Providence, held in the guild rooms of All Saints Church.

1871

Rev. C. C. Luther, A. M., for the past eighteen months pastor at North Lyme, Conn., has accepted a unanimous call to the First Baptist Church at Lyme, and took up the duties of the pastorate there March 15. The year and a half of country life having fully restored health impaired by severe work as an Evangelist. Mr. Luther hopes as opportunity offers to again resume in part evangelistic work in which for many years he has been eminently successful.

1872

The edifice of the First Baptist Church at Atlanta, Ga., of which Rev. William W. Landrum, D. D., is pastor, has been sold to the Government for about $100,000. A new post office will be erected on the site. The church is one of the largest and most influential in the South.

1873

Rev. Benjamin A. Greene, D. D., Brown, 1874, has prepared, for private circulation, a biography of his brother, the late Stephen Greene, of the class of 1873. The work is clear, discriminating and affectionate, and portrays the life of an able and noble son of Brown, a leader in business and an efficient church member. Following the biography is a full report of the memorial services at the Newton Centre church, and a selection of editorial articles and personal tributes bearing upon Mr. Greene's career. By those who were acquainted with Mr. Greene in undergraduate days or were associated with him in later years, this book will be highly prized.

1874

In the suit of the Bay State Gas Company against Lawson, Weidenfeld & Co., James E. Leach was appointed a receiver for certain securities.

1876

Lieutenant Charles H. Burritt is chief of the Mining Bureau, Department of the Interior, Philippine Islands. His office is in Manila.

1878

It was generally understood that, in the event of the creation of another supreme court judgeship in Rhode Island by the legislature which adjourned a few days ago, Judge William H. Sweetland of the sixth district court, Providence, would be elected to the place. The bill for the enlargement failed, however, of passage.

1880

Edgar Perry, M. D., died suddenly at his home, 1120 Boylston street, Boston, April 7, of a paralytic shock. He had previously suffered a stroke, on Thanksgiving Day, 1901, but had recovered sufficiently to take an active part in conducting his hospital and his practice. He was the son of Irah and Emily Read Perry. He was born at the ancestral home at Rehoboth, Mass., October 19, 1855. From 1880 to 1887 he was the proprietor and manager of the *Attleboro Chronicle*. In 1887 he went West and joined the staff of the *Cleveland Leader*, but in a few years returned to the East and joined the staff of the *Boston Herald*. He subsequently took up the study of medicine and was graduated at the Harvard Medical School in 1898. Almost immediately after receiving his degree he began the practice of medicine at 1120 Boylston street, Boston, when he soon established a most successful private hospital. He was a member of the Massachusetts Medical Society and of the Boston Medical Society. Mr. Perry was twice married, in 1888 to Emma E. Dwight, in 1898 to Emma J. Gordon. He is survived by his wife and three children by his first marriage.

1880

Charles Scribner's Sons have issued a book entitled " A History of the Babylonian and Assyrians" by George Stephen Goodspeed, Ph. D., professor of ancient history in the University of Chicago. The volume is an addition to the Historical Series for Bible Students edited by Professors Kent and Sanders of Yale University. A reviewer in the *Nation* of March 19 pronounced it "the best condensed history of Babylonia and Assyria yet published."

1884

W. M. P. Bowen of Providence has been reelected captain of Company A, First Light Infantry.

1886

Professor George G. Wilson ' to have charge of the courses on international law at the United States Naval War College at Newport during the summer of 1903.

1887

Henry Frederick Colwell is a member of the Boston Stock Exchange. His residence is in Jamaica Plain, Mass., 3 Greenough place.

Professor W. C. Bronson was one of the judges at the Putnam-Worcester high school debate at Putnam, Conn., April 24.

1888

Josiah Bartlett is the secretary and treasurer of the University Club which was recently organized at Poughkeepsie, N. Y.

Mrs. Barclay Hazard of New York has given $5,000 to the Hampton Institute, Virginia, to found an Indian Museum in memory of her brother, Eli Whitney Blake, II., who was for a time a teacher there.

1890

C. L. A. Heiser of Providence has been elected president of the Rumford Polo Club. Several Brown men are among the active members.

Rev. A. P. Bourne is taking a special course of study at the university.

1891

Professor Edwin G. Dexter of Illinois College has an article entitled " What is the best College?" in the April number of the *World's Work.*

Rev. F. H. Spear's new ministerial assignment by the Southern New England Conference of the Methodist Episcopal Church is at Woonsocket.

1892

At a special meeting of the vestry of Trinity Episcopal Church, Newport, April 23, Rev. Henry Morgan Stone, who has been the rector of the church for the last four years, tendered his resignation, owing to ill health. The vestry voted unanimously not to accept the resignation, but instead voted Mr. Stone a year's vacation.

Henry Kalloch Rowe is teacher of Latin and history in Frye's School for Boys in Boston.

1894

A son was born to Mr. and Mrs. Allan B. Morton in Atlanta, Ga., April 9. The child has been named Allan B. Morton, Jr. Mr. Morton is adjunct professor of mathematics and dean of the preparatory department in the Georgia School of Technology.

Fred Tenney is captain of the Boston National League nine.

1894

President M. E. Woolley of Mount Holyoke College addressed a large audience at Hartford a few days ago on " The Power of the Beautiful in Education."

1895

" John Burroughs has been expressing his mind about ' real and sham natural history,' and various writers of ' nature stories' will find this article in the current *Atlantic Monthly* unpalatable, says the *New York Sun.*

" Mr. Burroughs knows a thing or two about nature himself and the psychological studies of woodchucks and possums have goaded him into speech. He lets C. G. D. Roberts and William Davenport Hurlbert down easily, even praises them, with reservations, and he has an exceedingly good word for Dallas Lore Sharp, but falls upon Ernest Thompson Seton and belabors him merrily and the Rev. William Long's animal stories are apparently too much for his respect for the cloth."

Of Mr. Sharp's work Mr. Burroughs writes, ' Another book that I have read with genuine pleasure is Mr. Dallas Lore Sharp's Wild Life near Home, — a book full of charm and of real observation; the fruit of a deep and abiding love of Nature, and of power to paint her as she is." And again, the veteran naturalist thus comments : " Of all the nature-books of recent years, I look upon Mr. Sharp's as the best ; but in reading it, one is keenly aware of the danger that is always lurking near the essay naturalist, — lurking near me as well as Mr. Sharp, — the danger of making too much of what we see and describe, — of putting in too much sentiment, too much literature, — in short, of valuing things more for the literary effects we can get out of them than for themselves."

William Henry Atwood, for one year a member of the class of 1895, died at his home in New Bedford, Mass., Friday, April 3. Since leaving college he had been with the Morse Twist Drill and Machine Company of New Bedford.

1896

Miss Elizabeth Edwards of Livingston, Staten Island, N. Y., was married April 15, to Malcolm G. Chace, ex-1896 of Providence, at Livingston. The best man was William A. Larned, the national tennis champion, and among the ushers was Frank C. Hinckley, '91.

Haven Metcalf, who was lately called to the professorship of botany in Clemson College, South Carolina, received the degree of doctor of philosophy from the University of Nebraska last June.

A fellowship in history in the University of Chicago has been awarded to Marcus Wilson Jernegan for the academic year 1903-04.

1897

Horace G. Bissell has taken the place of P. H. Truman as first assistant clerk of the Common Pleas Division of the Supreme Court of Rhode Island.

Rev. F. J. C. Fitz Gerald is acting pastor of the Church of the Sacre Coeur, Northampton, Mass., during the absence of the French pastor. For the past few years Mr. Fitz Gerald has resided in Paris.

1898

A son was born to Mr. and Mrs. Dwight K. Bartlett of Detroit, Mich., on April 1. Mr. Bartlett has for several years resided in Detroit where he is in the employ of the American Blower Company.